WTH? Get Me Out of This Hell

Dr. Marlene Miles

Freshwater Press 2024
Freshwaterpress9@gmail.com

ISBN: 978-1-965772-26-3

Paperback Version

Table of Contents

Get Me Out of Hell

Freshwater

That's Life

The sad thing about being in hell, unless there is a guy with a red suit and a pitchfork, and flames everywhere is most people don't realize that is where they are. This is how it is described so often, so if hell is not really this or if hell doesn't really look like this, then how will we recognize it? And, how would we recognize if we are in hell or not? Even if we are told, say in a dream, that a place that we've encountered or found ourselves in is hell? Would we even believe it? Would we recognize it from descriptions we've heard about or read about? Would we remember it when we wake up?

It is not so much that God's judgements are subtle because they may not be subtle, but it is that the world has normalized hell, so if everyone else is doing it, everyone else is *like this*, everyone else is going through it--, then *that's life.*

No, that's hell.

God told Adam and Eve to not eat from the tree of the Knowledge of Good and evil, because on that day you will surely die. So, the devil enticed Eve to eat and then Eve gave to Adam from that "tree" and they surely died. You may say they didn't die, they were still walking around and living and being and doing, and even having kids.

None of us can call God a liar; God cannot lie. If God said they would die, they died. They didn't die physically, they died spiritually.

God forbid: yea, let God be true, but every man a liar; (Romans 3:4A)

They died. Not only did they die spiritually, but because of sin, they also were captured by the enemy because the enticement to sin was a trap, and they stepped right into it. Eve first. Then she recruited Adam. Sin begets sin; sinners recruit others to sin. Looking with his natural eyes, Adam betrayed himself by seeing with his own eyes that Eve had taken of that Tree and *didn't die*. What must Adam have been thinking? Was he thinking that God was joking or being overly dramatic? Natural eyes lie. Adam's natural eyes lied and told him that Eve was alive.

But she was dead.

And soon he would be also.

Yet the devil said that they wouldn't die--, and Eve is still alive. Careful! When you begin to believe the devil that is the first step in the path to hell.

When it is only important to be physically alive, forgetting that we are spirits, and we live in a spiritual world, and everything is spiritual is a huge mistake. Carnal people only care about what they look like, what they have, how they feel. What about the spirit man, does he get any consideration? God had just breathed life into Adam & Eve a couple of chapters ago, but each had already killed their spirit man inside of them.

Does anyone else now wonder where Cain got the idea or the wherewithal or the impetus to *murder* Abel? In three chapters, Adam and Eve had become spirit killers, soul killers, even though their flesh defied death—for now. Over and over I've heard pastors and teachers say that Cain committed the first murder. Did he? Cain's birth father and mother were both spiritually dead when they had him. The Bible doesn't say that God killed them. It doesn't say that the devil killed them. Yet, they were. Sin killed them, but they did it to themselves, making themselves the killers.

Sin was in Cain's foundation, and he gave into its impulses.

Behold, I was shapen in iniquity; and in sin did my mother conceive me. (Psalm 41:5)

Isn't that the story of Cain and all of us who were born after the Fall of man?

Innocence Lost

One of the things we love about babies and children is their innocence. When innocence is lost, we think about people in a different way, we see people differently. That is because **to lose innocence a person has to have gained a knowledge of evil**.

Sometimes we call innocence naivete and that is blissful, after all. When one can go through life and not have to look over his shoulder to see if someone is chasing you, or animals are against you or feel paranoid or post-traumatic stress about things that have happened to you then you have avoided the knowledge of evil. Anyone who knows nothing about evil is a happy person.

Soldiers get combat pay because of the dangers of where they are stationed or fighting. They see a lot of evil, when you see evil you get to know it but the real KNOWLEDGE of evil is carnal knowledge.

Do I mean sex?

Sometimes.

But experiencing evil is hard to *un*-experience, that's why in the world people go through years, even a lifetime of psychotherapy to get over childhood, early adult, or even wartime traumas, be they emotional, physical, sexual or of any kind.

They have taken from that "tree" or in the case of many soldiers and wartime survivors have had the fruit that they should not have tasted forced on them. Your little sister or brother, they are adorable, and you would do anything for them. But once they start their rebellion, disobedience, and willful sin life, you are not so adoring, are you? They are not so cute, are they? No, they are hiding and sneaking and trying, like Adam to cover up or get away with sin—**the knowledge of evil**. There is no place in man to store that knowledge and that is why the knowledge of evil disrupts a man so. It disrupts his spirit, his soul and even his flesh.

Once I was enticed to sin and it was a real enticement--, trust me, folks. But I knew that in my head there was no place to store the information that I would gain from participating in this sin. Some people believe they can forget their sin. I'm more like David in that my sin is ever before me. If you have the Holy Spirit, He will bring all things back to your remembrance. As long as that sin is unrepented sin, it will keep coming back into your memory. Sin is usually something you want to do, and therefore you may want to remember that time, not forget it.

I had absolutely no place within my being to store the experience or the data that I would download from the **knowledge** of this transgression. So, I didn't do it. I was fully aware that it was sin so it would have changed me dramatically; it may have ruined me, completely. I didn't do it; I ran from it. Thank the Lord.

It is the innocence that we love. That innocence is divine to us. It is when the innocence is lost that we don't esteem people the same way.

Just as looking on things we should not look on, we cannot **unsee** what we've seen, we cannot *un*-sin and regain innocence – at least not on our own and sometimes never in the eyes of other human beings. And we cannot send knowledge back to the sender. It's not actually as though someone sent the knowledge of evil to you, sometimes you go and get it. Once you get it, that knowledge of evil usurps innocence and takes over the spot where Innocence used to reign. Now you're different.

You've either heard it said or said it yourself, "She used to be such a sweet girl, but then she *changed*." Yes, she did—she took of that "tree." It's as though we can tell, no matter how much people tried to hide that they've begun to have sex, or commit other sins, for example. People change. Sin changes people. Sin and its guilt makes people hide, mean, cruel, sneaky, prideful, or arrogant –, any number of emotions. It depends on the person; but we all change. Sin changes people and really, sin changes everything.

You've heard people say that others are dead to them, as in dead *in sin.* It's as though they see some of it--, but not all of what is going on. There is a reproach that the devil puts on people when they sin, they lose favor, they lose benefits and blessings, and it is seen in the natural. Even if it is not really *seen,* it is felt, or sensed. Sin chases favor out the door. Reproach from God translates to reproach in the natural from man; God hates sin, but He still loves the sinner who will repent.

Yes, we, who are like God celebrate innocence and we disdain sin, as we should. If you are not being celebrated, appreciated, or respected, that could be a sign that you have a invisible, spiritual mark of reproach, rejection or hatred on you. If you do, then that indicates that you are in captivity in the spirit. Whatever happens on Earth happens in the spirit realm first.

If you have to fight for every little thing you get in life, you are probably in captivity. Are you rejected for no reason even when you meet brand new people? Are you hated, stared at, treated poorly even though you are being as respectful, kind, and nice as you can be?

You are most likely marked with a mark because you are in captivity. Mankind is not designed to live this life in captivity--, that's not really living.

Perhaps we should visit the definition of **life** or the description of hell and compare the two. Else, how will be know what to accept and what to reject?

This is life and it is an abundant life; accept this. Chase after this. Embrace this:

If you fully obey the Lord your God and carefully follow all his commands I give you today, the Lord your God will set you high above all the nations on earth. All these blessings will come on you and accompany you if you obey the Lord your God:

You will be blessed in the city and blessed in the country.

The fruit of your womb will be blessed, and the crops of your land and the young of your livestock—the calves of your herds and the lambs of your flocks.

Your basket and your kneading trough will be blessed.

You will be blessed when you come in and blessed when you go out.

The Lord will grant that the enemies who rise up against you will be defeated before you. They will come at you from one direction but flee from you in seven. The Lord will send a blessing on your barns and on everything you put your hand to. The Lord your God will bless you in the land he is giving you. The Lord will establish you as his holy people, as he promised you on oath, if you keep the commands of the Lord your God and walk in obedience to him. Then all the peoples on earth will see that you are called by the name of the Lord, and they will fear you. The Lord will grant you abundant prosperity—in the fruit of your womb, the young of your livestock and the crops of your ground—in the land he swore to your ancestors to give you. The Lord will open the heavens, the storehouse of his bounty, to send rain on your land in season and to bless all the work of your hands. You will lend to many nations but will borrow from none. The Lord will make you the head, not the tail. If you pay attention to the commands of the Lord your God that I give you this day and carefully follow them, you will always be at the top, never at the bottom. Do not turn aside from any of the commands I give you today, to the right or to the left, following other gods and serving them. (Deuteronomy 28:1-15 NIV)

Following these commands is the recipe for an abundant life. This is what living is supposed to be about.

The thief cometh not, but for to steal, and to kill, and to destroy: I am come that they might have life, and that they might have it more abundantly. (John 10:10)

No, That's Hell

If we keep explaining away **hell** as *just life*, we will never try to get out of it. We can see others really going through life. No, that's hell that your friends or relatives may be experiencing. Still if they are going through it, they should be going *through* it and not camping out there or moving in.

If we can't see hell in our own lives, in ourselves, can we not see it in another? We wag our heads at the behavior of people, who are still people--, for the most part, but they are in hell. That is why they behave as sinners, criminals, and hellions. They are doing what they are supposed to be doing--, and that is sinning.

The preparations of the heart in man, and the answer of the tongue, *is* from the LORD. All the ways of a man *are* clean in his own eyes; but the LORD weigheth the spirits. Commit thy works unto the LORD, and thy thoughts shall be established. The

LORD hath made all *things* for himself: yea, even the wicked for the day of evil. (Proverbs 16:1-4)

This is why we don't war against flesh and blood. God's people weren't made *like* this or *for* this--, they are being **made** to behave this way. Hell and the *spirits* and powers of Hell influence or coerce people to behave unlike *people* and behave like demons.

That's Hell.

I am ever convinced that the news we see on TV is such bad news because it appears to be about people behaving badly, but if we look very deeply, we will see it is *evil spirits* in people inducing them to behave badly. Haven't you noticed the bad people are all the same kind of bad, no matter what town, city, or country they live in? Yes, they are being influenced by wicked powers from the second heaven. It doesn't matter what you look like or what language you speak, if you are human, you will be impacted in the same way by wicked powers in the heavens. For example, there are happy drunks and mean drunks; they all act one of those two ways when under the influence. The influence of what? Alcohol, which is *spirits*.

If a person is behaving like a hellion, it is because they are made to behave that way. Did they choose it? Possibly, but sometimes captivity is chosen for a person. If the family you're born in is in captivity, then so are you, it's called collective captivity. The company you keep, you actually choose they could all be captives as well. Do you think the visitors or denizens in a crack house are in captivity? Yes, they all are; that's why they are there. Anyone who is committing a sin and really doesn't want to do that sin--, they want out of that lifestyle, that person is in captivity.

The Curse of the Law:
But the Lord God called to the man, "Where are you?"

He answered, "I heard you in the garden, and I was afraid because I was naked; so I hid."

And he said, "Who told you that you were naked? Have you eaten from the tree that I commanded you not to eat from?"

The man said, "The woman you put here with me—she gave me some fruit from the tree, and I ate it."

Then the Lord God said to the woman, "What is this you have done?"

The woman said, "The serpent deceived me, and I ate." (Genesis 3:9-13 NIV)

Who told you that you were naked? No one had to tell Adam that he was now naked because he had been created "good", but now he has experienced evil; therefore, he now knows good **and** evil, which the serpent had told him would happen. Well, it happened. Evil is the serpent and all that are with him and follow him. Adam and Eve knew no evil and knew nothing *of* evil, they were created perfectly by God. Now that they know evil, they cannot *un*-**know** it.

In the natural we have to learn that some things are not a defense. *Who* induced you to sin is not material; God will deal with that person, just as he did in subsequent verses with the Serpent. The Serpent got his own curse but that did not preclude Eve from receiving a different curse, or Adam from being now under the curse of the Law. Nor did it stop Adam and Eve from **knowing** evil.

To the woman he said,

"I will make your pains in childbearing
very severe;
with painful labor you will give birth to
children.
Your desire will be for your husband,
and he will rule over you."

To Adam he said, "Because you listened to your wife and ate fruit from the tree about which I commanded you, 'You must not eat from it,'

"Cursed is the ground because of you;
through painful toil you will eat food
from it
all the days of your life.
It will produce thorns and thistles for you,
and you will eat the plants of the field.
By the sweat of your brow
you will eat your food
until you return to the ground,
since from it you were taken;
for dust you are
and to dust you will return."

Adam named his wife Eve, because she would become the mother of all the living. (Genesis 3: 16-20).

Folks, God just spoke the Curse of the Law to Eve and then to Adam and since they are one (married) and both of mankind, and they both sinned, they share in the Curse. Additionally, since Eve is the mother of all living, we will be born with her iniquity because of her sin. In between, God spoke Satan's curse, but it is not the scope of this volume.

Looking over those verses, if you've got any of this going on in your life, you are under the Curse of the Law. As a woman, because of Eve, you will experience the following:

- Pain in childbearing: Curse of the Law.
- Desire for the husband, yet he rules over you: Curse of the Law.
  Adam's Curse:
- Man's food will now come from the ground.

At first they were able to eat of any **tree** in the Garden except one. Now man has to bend his back and also bow to the ground in order to eat. Man must now bow, whereas before he was **upright**, walking and feeding from trees. (This adds insight to walking upright before the Lord. Walking upright means before sin, or absent sin if we are also in Christ and redeemed from sin and death then we are restored to our created position and authority.)

- Cursed is the ground; you will have painful toil, but this is how you will eat all the days of your life.
- The ground will produce thorns and thistles.
- Sweat and toil to get the land to produce so you can eat.

Saints of God, have you considered that the ground, the Earth, even all of creation responds differently to the created and perfect man than it does to a sinner who has lost his position, dominion, authority and possibly his glory and crown of honor? If you bend down to cultivate the soil, to plant and garden and grow things, how will your crown stay on your head? Seems that crown was lost in the fall of man. Man fell and his crown of honor also fell off his head and was taken.

As part of the Curse of the Law, do the things that God created to show forth His glory and for the use of His people still do what you say do? Do those things still obey the voice of your commands? Do those things still produce for you? Do those things still produce what God said they would produce for *His people* for a people who have lost their position and their authority? My Bible says that the ground was cursed for the sake of man because of their sin. So not only would they eat from the ground, it would be hard to do so.

The now un-innocent man is treated differently by creation and also by people, as you may have seen by the way you treat known sinners, and the way you too are treated as an unrepentant sinner, with guilt and having lost favor and position.

Let's say you give your American Express card to your child to go shopping; all is well. Now your child misbehaves in any number of ways, or in even one way, don't you cut off their credit? Yes you do. That American Express card will not yield benefits to the disobedient and rebellious child as it did for the child who would obey you.

Wouldn't the Earth be like (or better than) an American Express Card? First would we ever leave home without the Earth? No, unless we are astronauts, and even if we were, we'd be returning eventually. Don't we want the Earth to yield its increase to us? I mean, we have to eat. Isn't there no credit limit on the Earth, as long as it is not cursed, just as it is on the traditional American Express Card, as long as you are in good standing with them? There is no limit to what God will do for you as long as you are walking upright before Him. Now unto him that is able to do exceeding abundantly above all that we ask or think, according to the power that worketh in us, (Ephesians 3:20)

I'm saved, I am redeemed from the Curse of the Law, you may be saying as your defense.

Yes you are, but have you **enforced** the redemption against the one who wants you to remain under that curse? You must insist on it because the devil is counting on you not knowing that you are redeemed and walking in that.

Have you fully repented, because if you are cursed, then you are all the more *curse-able*. Have you sinned since you've been saved? Have you sinned since salvation and have not repented? Are you a carnal Christian? Are you CINO--, Christian in Name Only? Have you sinned since yesterday? Last night? An hour ago?

For all have sinned, and come short of the glory of God; (Romans 3:23)

The whole world is a stage, and everyone is playing a part. We may all think that we are on that stage of our own free will and autonomy, but we should think again. We are beautiful and handsome clay vessels that the Lord has made to carry His glory, but if we are taken over, we may purposefully or inadvertently carry the devil's inglorious nature. In addition, the devil may have helped himself by corrupting our family's foundation through our ancestors, that neither than nor us even know anything about. Well, we don't know until life doesn't work for us as it should, then we have to figure out why. All day and all night we are getting suggestions and influences. So as we trot the boards of the stage *of life* what are we doing? What are we saying? Who told or influenced us to do or say that?

Someone just asked me a bizarre question that surely came from her grandmother or a friend's ancestor. The question made no sense and does not bear repeating, but that question is probably part of the conversation that happened or happens in the house that person grew up in. My point is that parents and ancestors will write our scripts for our unseen lives. If we do nothing about it, by being saved and fully in Christ, that is what we will walk out--, their bizarre thoughts and expectations on life, rather than what God says.

So, my parents can live through me?

Yup, they do, every day of the week, unless you get a new Father, new parentage and you are fully *in* and walking upright before the Lord. In this way you take on the nature of Christ and you do not fulfill the often misguided words of ancestors, forefathers, and other evil spiritual *influencers*.

So-called self-made men believe themselves captains of their own destinies are really not. We are free in Christ, else we are slaves to the flesh, sin, and the devil. It is spiritual powers stronger than they are, or think they are, or know themselves to be are really their puppet masters, unless they are in Christ. Whatever they worship owns them. Whatever they worship rules them. Whatever they worship influences them. Whatever they worship runs their life.

Then there are those who believe they haven't chosen anything or anyone to worship.

But they have.

Man is created to worship; he will worship every waking moment and sometimes while he is asleep. There is a default on Earth, if you do not choose that you will worship God, then the default happens automatically. The default is the devil, it is the dark kingdom, and that is Hell. Hell is the path of almost no resistance, the devil, hell and his hellions influence mankind to resist God, the Kingdom of Light, and godliness, fervently 24/7. They make it hard to do right and so easy to do wrong.

Enter ye in at the strait gate: for wide is the gate, and broad is the way, that leadeth to destruction, and many there be which go in thereat:
Because strait is the gate, and narrow is the way, which leadeth unto life, and few there be that find it. (Matthew 7:13-14)

Maybe you didn't choose. Sometimes it is who <u>chose</u> you. If you don't object to having been chosen, then that choice stands.

If Billy selected you for his dodgeball team and you say nothing, run over to Billy's side, then you are on that team. So it goes that whomever they have chosen, or who chose them, even centuries ago, through an evil or deceived ancestor, that is what stands. This is the hand that has been dealt to a human. If this were not so, then why would God be so forgiving of sins? He knows His creation and He knows that man was not made *for* that or to do *that*.

My defence is of God, which saveth the upright in heart. God judgeth the righteous, and God is angry with the wicked every day. (Proverbs 7:10-11)

It is why God is so angry with those who embrace the dark side on purpose. God chooses, as well: Jacob have I loved, Esau, I have hated. As it is written, Jacob have I loved, but Esau have I hated. (Romans 9:13)

I am *in* Jacob. How about *you*?

Living Hell

You've heard people say that something was a living hell. What can that possibly mean?

Sadly, as we will discuss in the next few chapters, there is hell for the living. There is hell for people who are still alive. It is subjective as we will find out; one man's hell may be lots of fun for another who is fully demonized. A hellion may think hellish talk, hellish conditions, and other hellish people are fun or their cup of tea, until they find out that they are not on the administration side of that living hell, but they will be victims, themselves. A sadist would like to administer hell to others, but they can't take it themselves. In the natural this is often seen as witches and spell casters send curses to people, to make the lives of others a living hell. But, when those curses ricochet, the witches don't like it very much.

A living hell is A continuing state of extreme pain, punishment, suffering,
or torment with no seeming chance of reprieve. People want this for their enemies, but we are not supposed to want this for other people. In our warfare prayer verbiage, we can be very violent against spiritual entities and enemies, but not against flesh and blood, according to the Word of God which governs Christians.

Let **everything** that is within me praise the Lord. We must **make** ourselves praise the Lord, we command ourselves to praise the Lord, we command our flesh, our soul and our spirit man to praise the Lord. When parts of us are not praising it is because we either won't or can't. Those are the parts that are on lockdown. What do I mean?

Some who go into prayer cannot press in. Some who go into praise or worship yet cannot get into the presence of God. Is it because we don't know how or is it because God is rejecting us or is it because there are parts of us that are not cooperating or able? Are parts of us spiritually handicapped or soulishly handicapped, or already worshipping something else? Or, simply on lockdown?

For example, what we look like on the outside says who or what we are worshipping. Now, I'm not making fun of anyone at all, any examples are only examples. A person with diamonds or jewelry on every finger and sometimes more than one ring on a finger is worshipping?

_____(you fill in the blank). We go to the Bible to see where that is or where God said to do that to find out.

Okay, I checked, it is not in there in that way.

The person who has on 8 layers of makeup. The person whose hair is a whole altar--, they want their style to be so different that they must get attention. What influences a person to dress like a street walker? It's not God; know that. When you are dressed like that, another strange altar, who do you think will run up to worship you, or take advantage of you. Strange people. Strangers who offer strange worship. Is that what you are looking to accomplish? That style of dress does not foster respect from others. Dressing like that, one cannot then wonder why they never meet *good people.* Your demonic lockdown precludes you from meeting good people, marrying types—it is part of your hell. The demonic lockdown influences your outfits and what you look like.

You have got to pray to get out of hell while you can. Do the work of getting out of hell while it is day, for the night comes, when permanent hell arrives there is no getting out of this.

The person who has soaked in fragrance so that the people they meet in life start sneezing are influenced by *what* to do that? In my office building, I can get on the elevator and tell you who was last on it, just from what it smells like in there.

The person who has or wears excess anything when God says let your moderation be shown is not obeying God. Is it because they won't? Is it because they *can't?* When God says let your adornment be on the inside. Might we surmise that excesses are demonic, and devil influenced? God says do not store up for yourselves treasures that rust and can get moth-eaten. If we are doing the opposite of what God says, then who is influencing that?

Now, if we are obeying, then there is a part of us that has rebelled to the Word of God. There is a part of us that is weak enough that it will do what the enemy or enemies of God say do rather than obey our Father.

All the while we are at church, and we *say* we are Christians; we *seem* to be or want to be *seen* as Christians.

If we are being **forced** to disobey God, then the part that is disobedient is in hell.

There is hell for the living; it can be and should be temporary if anyone finds themselves there. And there is hell for the dead; it is permanent, and you don't want to go there if you have been told about it. You also don't want to go to Hell for the dead if you've ever experienced hell for the living.

Yet some are fascinated with horror houses and Halloween. One woman told me she was drawn to Salem, Massachusetts because of the mediums in her family.

I said, *Witches*?

She said, Well, there are good witches and bad witches.

I said, There are no good witches.

She insisted. **She's wrong.** She is deceived. Find that in the Bible and tell me, please.

To know the **knowledge** of witchcraft to do it, to practice it is the same as eating the apple from the tree of the Knowledge of Good & Evil.

This deceived woman is on lockdown and must do what is in her foundation, what is in her blood, what is in her instructions to do. This is what her ancestors have left her, and they've convinced her that it is good, or special. It is the knowledge of evil and it is BAD, very bad.

Now the works of the flesh are manifest, which are these; Adultery, fornication, uncleanness, lasciviousness,

Idolatry, **witchcraft**, hatred, variance, emulations, wrath, strife, seditions, heresies,

Envyings, murders, drunkenness, revellings, and such like: of the which I tell you before, as I have also told you in time past, that they which do such things shall not inherit the kingdom of God. *(Galatians 5:19-21, emphasis, mine)*

The only way out is Jesus Christ.

If there are no "good witches" in the Bible, then where wood "good witches" come from? TV? Movies? Make believe. *Uh huh.*

Exactly, there are no good witches.

Crowd Captivity

However, those who relish evil, those who enjoy it, whether they see that they are doing it or not, are living very dangerously. Those who follow crowds who are evil, whether they see it or not, should be feeling the burn because they are already in hell and running towards it by their own actions, thoughts, ideas, plans, and agreements.

Those who get caught up in certain crowds or in mob mentality, and want to do damage to something, someone, or a people group are in captivity of hell or running by the broad way straight into it. God didn't say don't forgive people; the devil sponsors that. God didn't say get revenge on people; vengeance is the Lord's. God didn't say to mock people and make fun of them; that is the devil's work. God didn't say hate the stranger or be wicked to the poor or the widow; God said quite the opposite. God didn't say just because everybody is doing it, or chanting it, or agreeing on something evil then it is no longer evil; it is still evil. Now God will have to judge all in the crowd, or in the mob.

The Bible tells us not to cause strife and dissension and that all these things are works of the flesh. Those who are compelled to join evil groups and working the flesh are doing the opposite of what the Word says. Those who are in a crowd or mob working the flesh are in hell. Further, if they want to remain linked together, they are in a gang up.

They are in the same category (verse) with witchcraft. Read it again.

Idolatry, **witchcraft**, hatred, variance, emulations, wrath, strife, seditions, heresies,

Envyings, murders, drunkenness, revellings, and such like: of the which I tell you before, as I have also told you in time past, that they which do such things **shall not inherit the kingdom of God.** (Galatians 5:20-21, *emphasis, mine*)

Do they not realize it? Do they not see it? Do they not see themselves?

If they do and willfully continue, the living hell that they are in is at risk of becoming permanent hell.

What part of the person who is blatantly disobeying the Word of God is also at the same time godly? Praying effectual prayers? Worshipping the Lord? Even able to get into the presence of God?

I have a brother who used to tell me to do wrong things and challenge me that I was afraid to do those things. What things? Steal, for example. Young and dumb, I did it once to prove that I could; I stole a quarter, from my dad. As soon as I did, my brother told on me to get me into trouble. He thought this was fun. I was totally confused when he did this because, he's my brother, and he was the one who told me to do it, but he is now tattling. That made no sense to me.

Was my brother saved? You tell me. Did God tell my brother to do this? You know the answer.

WHO are you listening to? Your big brother? A fearless leader? A real pastor or a fake one? You must discern and you will know them by their fruit.

If you are listening to the devil, he is the Accuser of the Brethren. If it is a human who is the mouthpiece of the devil, he or she will talk just like the devil. As soon as you sin, the devil is right at the Throne of God tattling on you, and worse, trying to get a judgment against you to get permission to *lock you up*. If you sin or commit a crime, no matter what was said before, the devil's mouthpiece will quickly disavow knowledge of who you are and why you did what you did, even if they told you to do it, or provoked you to do it.

I was nine years old when I learned this. I am far from 9 years old now, but I believe I am lamenting that loss of innocence because it changed me. It changed how I must see and deal with my own brother and others like him. Yes, I learned from it, but I was much happier when I didn't **know** that evil—either the evil of committing the sin or the crime, nor having to remember now that my brother is capable of this, and I can't trust him as I used to, when I was innocent, and also thought that he was *innocent*.

Lord, forgive me. Did I ever repent of this? Lord, forgive me for stealing that quarter and also trying to hide it and get away with it. If memory serves, I believe I put that quarter back, but I never admitted that I had stolen it. Even though I put it back, that doesn't change the fact that I had stolen it and tried, like Adam and Eve, to hide that fact. Lord, forgive me, in the Name of Jesus.

As a child, since my elder brother told me to do something, that does not make it right or make me innocent if I actually did the crime or the sin. Therefore, we must consider who in Earth is telling us to do things, even if it is a person with authority over us. Also, we must discern who, spiritually, is encouraging or influencing us to do things. Those sins are only going to get us in trouble and that trouble often is hell because the part that you sin with is now available for hell, living hell. Temporary or permanent, but hell. Temporary because hopefully we will realize that we were wrong and see the error of our ways and repent quickly and be restored back into right relationship with God. All parts of us, our whole soul must be back in right step with the Lord, not just the part that people <u>see</u>.

Flesh Hell

Flesh Hell-- no, not *fresh hell*, although that could be a thing, but flesh hell.

Can we not feel that our flesh is in hell? Haven't you heard anyone say that something *hurts like hell*? What do you think they mean? It is when pain or discomfort hits our flesh that we acutely realize that we are somehow experiencing *hell*.

Shall we not realize that we are in hell, if we are? At least that body part is, when our flesh feels it. Shall I say, finally <u>feels</u> it.

You've seen in movies that a witch or voodoo priest may make effigy dolls, voodoo figures and do things to it but people who are under their curse feel it. That is a crazy spiritual thing that happens in the spirit, by demonic power. It affects people in the natural, often in the flesh. Sometimes it can affect the mind, for example to cause confusion, madness and other soul afflictions. That is a witch agreeing with the second heaven that so-and-so should be hurt or suffer pain, or even be dead.

Witchcraft is very powerful when it is unopposed. When someone has gone through the trouble to make up an effigy, full sized or miniature, of another to torment and torture or murder them, this is quite serious. Do you think they've made up that doll and that people have been doing this for ages if it doesn't work? Do you think they'd keep doing it if it is only make-believe? Do you think that God has a punishment for witches, if witches don't *exist*?

So, this evil spiritual activity is happening. All the while that doll is being made the intended victim doesn't feel anything, but once those spiritual actions are performed on the doll--, by the time it hits the flesh of a real human being, oh, that non-believing person, or dry, non-praying Christian victim will know it.

Flesh is slower than spirit and slower than the vibrations of the soul. I believe manifestations have been in the spirit and then in the soul before it finally hits the flesh. Therefore, we missed it. We missed the signal in the spirit, in our spirit, then we missed the soul afflictions. But the flesh – where we primarily live, especially as carnal Christians, we felt that. We saw that. We noticed that.

When in the spirit you suddenly don't feel like praying anymore. You don't feel like reading the Bible. You may be distracted; you have an urge to sin. Or, you are making excuses not to serve God such as you are too busy, or the church or the pastor are getting on your nerves. You may suddenly feel or be overcome with problems or taken by sleep wave. Those are spiritual manifestations that may have been missed or ignored.

Sleep wave? You thought you were just tired and started going to bed earlier, taking B12 drops or added beetroot powder to your morning smoothie. None of that helped because the problem was spiritual, not physiological. People miss bizarre or important dreams that are given to them to alert them to upcoming attacks, issues, or even doom; but do they even notice or acknowledge dreams? Worse, when your dreams are missing or totally ignored, suspect real spiritual trouble is afoot.

Something is up in the spirit, but did we notice? Dreams are wiped or ignored, not interpreted or interpreted incorrectly. God is trying to tell us something. You thought you saw a shadow in your house but maybe not really. You talked yourself out of it.

That was a *monitoring spirit*, a *follow-follow spirit* and it was sizing you up for an attack. It was evaluating the best time, the best day, the best way, to spiritually attack you, but did you do anything about it?

Right when you saw it is when you could have nipped the whole thing in the bud. Later, you got agitated, nervous for no apparent reason – the attack has started, and it may have hit your soul, your emotions. What did you do then? Anything?

Next thing you know there is a flesh response

Now, how long it takes to go from a spiritual attack to a person feeling it in their soul, or in their flesh is particular to your case; there is no set time. So pay attention. This is what discernment is for and about, it is to see and know things while they are in the spiritual mode and keep them from manifesting in the Earth, in your soul and in your flesh.

The stronger your spirit man is, the more you can ward off spiritual attacks, if they hit, you can fight and win quickly, even sending them back to sender. Conversely, if your spirit man is weak, those attacks may land, you may feel them, and you may not endure them well.

I heard a prophet once say that when something spiritual (an issue, disease, disorder., etc) gets into the third generation of a family, it's really *in there*. It is deeply embedded in their bloodline by then. Looking at three's it may be wise for us to say, spirit, soul, and body, by the time it gets to the body, it's really *in there*. It surely will be harder to get rid of once it afflicts the body because many times you just don't feel like doing what you need to do to get rid of the problem. Worse, by the time it hits the flesh, it has taken a position in the spirit, and taken up residence in the soul and now the three-pronged attack has hit the flesh. This is a wowie!

How could one end up in Flesh Hell, and even while still alive?

Satanic prison of the flesh. The people are still alive but are imprisoned in hell. I've not been there, with awareness in the dream or in the spirit, but this is how it is reported by so many who have had NDE's (near death experiences). The report is that hell is vast. Which hell? We don't know, but that it is also full of people. So full. Too full.

One human in hell must grieve the heart of God.

In these living hells a person is told that they must never pray or sing adoration and praise, only do what they are told. So at the flesh level the demons who enforce that make you more fleshy, lazy, more carnal, and anti-God, anti-prayer, anti-giving, unholy--, more carnal.

You eat what you are told to eat. I've thought about this for years --, cravings. Why do you want the same food over and over? Why do you *only* want that food and nothing more? Nothing different? Nothing new? Why do you binge on things that are no good for you? The demons in your soul or the ones in the spirit are directing you to hurt your own flesh by overeating or eating food that is not good for you. They don't just want food, they want alcohol and drugs too, if they can get you to imbibe and take them.

Killing you softly? Killing you slowly.

That which I would do, I find myself not doing that, but that which I do not want to do, that is what I'm doing.

I don't really understand myself, for I want to do what is right, but I don't do it. Instead, I do what I hate. But if I know that what I am doing is wrong, this shows that I agree that the law is good. So I am not the one doing wrong; it is sin living in me that does it.

And I know that nothing good lives in me, that is, in my sinful nature] I want to do what is right, but I can't. I want to do what is good, but I don't. I don't want to do what is wrong, but I do it anyway. But if I do what I don't want to do, I am not really the one doing wrong; it is sin living in me that does it. (Romans 7:15-20)

Apostle Paul said that. A true man of God. This is captivity, when your own free will is taken away from you and you are sinning again when you didn't want to sin. You eat when you want to fast. You are overeating when you want to diet. You are drinking alcohol or relapsing into some other behavior when you didn't want to.

You are chasing women and sex or men and sex, but you feel so guilty after you have done that. Folks, those are true signs of captivity.

How is anyone a captive? They've been apprehended, arrested. Handcuffed, possibly shackled, locked up. Caged.

You can't do what you want to do. You have a desire and a heart to do right – the spirit is willing, but the flesh is weak. The flesh has been beaten down, weakened. There is a demonic charge or authority over the flesh, lording over it commanding it to do this, that, or the other, and you are either their compliant or forced *slave*. Like a zombie, you do what you are told and you don't even know why.

Why don't you pray in your waking life?

"It is forbidden to pray here; they just tell us to sleep," said the person who had the near-death experience and the visit to the hells.

Sleep wave comes over you when you want to pray. When you want to read the Bible, you find yourself asleep. Sleep wave is demonic, but it is a real thing. Sleep wave comes over you because they told you to sleep, and you are captive. Do you see what is happening here? We see this a lot in older people who fall asleep anytime during the day. Absent of having stayed up all night with the party crowd or the grown ups, that is captivity, directing you to sleep--, so you do. It's not that you've old or super-old, it's sleep wave. It's captivity. It's so you are not productive, not energetic and driving towards your goals, Purpose, and destiny.

Those who fight it usually fight it with food, drugs, pills, or vitamins – all of which cost money, but if used incorrectly can throw your whole system out of balance.

You see some elderly just sitting in their chair sleeping away in the middle of the day, while some seniors are out there doing life. But the devil can't kill you because of God. Because God has more plans for you? Yes. Because God has more things for you to do? Yes. Because God, in His Mercy knows that senior, that elderly person can still be saved, and you are preserved for the saving of your soul. God knows there is still Purpose in that older gent or lady, so even if you are in captivity, God knows that you can come out. God may even know that you will come out—but will you do what is necessary to get out of that particular hell?

You sleep, but it is not unto death.

You sleep, because you are in some hellish gulag. You sleep because you must for the sin that captured you and got you here. You sleep because of the iniquity of sin. And, you sleep because you are their prisoner, their slave; so you must do as they say.

For now.

But, as God brought the Hebrews out of slavery, a million or more of them, can He not also bring you out of captivity? You, just one solitary soul? Jesus said that the Father does not wish that even one would be lost. You may feel lost, but God knows where you are and He knows that you can come out. Repent; ask Him to deliver your soul from hell.

Everyone who is sleeping, or who sleeps a lot is not necessarily lazy; many are captives and must do as they are told--, they are told to sleep. This could be why many Christians sleep when they could be praying.

People who live by the flesh, are alive on Earth, but they are captive in Flesh Hell.

The guards or jailers prevent people from praying. These captives are in prison and may not even realize it, they just think that they are tired or feeling badly.

Others may think they are having fun and living it up, depending on what their demonic assignment is – right now. I still have the question of what would make one man have eight children by 5 different women, not be married to any of them and not have any money or means or desire to take care of the women or the children?

Repetitive sin is the cause of being here. Repetitive sin is the **result** of being here. That man is captive. Period.

To get out of there, he must confess sins and seek the Face of God in prayer.

In the natural you get punished for praying—that is if you do a little dab of praying. If you pray halfway, half-hearted or once or twice, the enemy will send in a deluge against you. They break cars, they mess with people's money, health and anything to make them uncomfortable, unprofitable, unsuccessful, even broke. If you are in captivity, prayer and calling on the Name of Jesus is the only way out, and you may have to do it over and over with determination and authority. Even if the enemy is trying to slay you, keep calling on the Name of the Lord.

Falling Apart

The devil is more subtle than many. The easiest captivity for the captor is when you don't even know that you are captive. When they let you keep some good things, you may not realize that the rest of you is under guard. I know a woman who believes herself to be very beautiful and she will tell you that of all her siblings, she's the pretty one. The rest of her life is a disaster, but she believes she is okay because she believes she's beautiful and she is sticking with that.

When the devil lets you keep one or two things that actually belong to you, those things belong to your peace. Don't get too complacent, don't get forlorn, don't be greedy, but where is the rest of all the Lord promised you. Let's review the promises to find out what you should have. If you never take inventory, how will you give thanks to

God who provided the good things in your life? If you never count your blessings, how will you know what you have? What are you supposed to have? Or, what is missing?

The devil is a legalist--, that's why lawyers can sometimes have a bad reputation because the letter of the law kills, but the Spirit of the law gives life. When observing the letter of the law folks like Pharisees and Sadducees are nit-picking and getting into the fine print and the fine-fine print of any matter, usually to catch someone in a lie, or in a crime. With the devil, the *crime* is spiritual, so it is a sin.

This means that the devil will have to go by the *Book*, whatever is allowed he will certainly use it or try to use it to harm his victim. So, for sin he will fling any of the following at you that he can, from Deuteronomy 28:15-68). I will summarize most of the verses, but in no particular order. You, however, should read that passage for yourself to get the full impact of it.

- Curses will overtake you.

That means that when people sling curses at you, they will **stick,** and what the witch or warlock wants to happen, you are at serious risk of it happening. If it is a physical attack, especially, it may feel as though you are *falling apart.* You may feel this way because the affliction is sudden and something else may have happened to you last week, especially something in your physical body.

- Any network of automatic arrows fired at me, let that network break and those arrows return to sender, in the Name of Jesus.

If you don't want to say return to sender then say,

- Any network of automatic arrows fired at me, lose your power, in the Name of Jesus.

If it seems that stuff keeps happening to you, all of a sudden, watch yourself--, watch your mouth. Don't let your mouth agree with the evil arrow. Don't agree with the curse. Don't agree with the bad thing that is happening to you. Send the evil arrow back and state the opposite of what the devil wanted to happen to you by stating what God says you are, by faith.

- There's nowhere to go to get away from the curse.
- Your money will be cursed.
- Children will be cursed, if you can even have any.

This is where the falling apart symptoms are usually noticed or spoken about, diseases come upon the cursed person. Inflammation, fever, mildew (fungus). Diseases that He put on the Egyptians to include incurable tumors, boils, festering sores, madness, blindness, and confusion.

- Losing spiritual battles, and therefore battles in the natural. Suddenly there are a lot of fires to put out. It never used to be like this.

I know. You weren't in captivity before where the devil can do almost anything to you. Didn't the devil keep doing stuff to Job? It wasn't like that for Job at

first, was it? No, it wasn't. Even Job
reminisced about the good old days.

> When I washed my steps with butter, and
> the rock poured me out rivers of oil; (Job
> 29:6)

The Bible doesn't read that Job was
captive, but we know that Satan got
permission from God to do all he did to Job.
If you're captive the devil had to get
permission from God--, that's why he keeps
accusing the brethren 24/7, to get judgments
against mankind so he can capture them and
steal, kill or destroy them. It's not as though
he has absconded with you; God knows
where you are. I'm sure God is not happy
with anyone being captive, but God cannot
lie. Therefore, if God says the wages of sin
is death, then it is. If God says if you eat of
that Tree you will die, then that is what
happens. If God says choose life because if
you choose sin, this, that and the other will
happen to you, it will.

But God still knows where you are.
God always knows where all of us are. Note
the wording of that verse: *If I make my bed
in hell.* This is the same as the writer

admitting to how he got in hell—he made his own bed there. Doesn't the saying go, *You made your bed, now you have to lie in it?*

If I ascend up into heaven, thou art there: if I make my bed in hell, behold, thou art there. (Psalm 139:8)

- If you are oppressed, feeling weighed down, stressed out, you are cursed.
- Anti-marriage is a curse. Husbands and wives will hate one another (Deuteronomy 28: 56)
- Your children will go into bondage, given to another *nation*. This is not always physical; it can be spiritual captivity as well. A *nation* can be an evil spiritual dominion or throne.
- The sights you see will drive you mad. (Deuteronomy 28:34). You can't unsee that stuff, so guard your eye-gates.
- You will be driven to servitude and slavery.
- Will live in an unknown land and be forced into more idolatry (Deuteronomy 28:36)

- Curses chase you, they pursue you until they overtake you and you will be destroyed—that is the enemy's desire against you. Who sends a curse just for fun or just to make you uncomfortable for a while? No, they either want destruction, or the power they are working with wants destruction. So, take this very seriously.
- Obey the Lord your God and observe the commands and decrees he gave you, and live! (Deuteronomy 28:45)
- Cursed to eat the fruit of your own womb and consume your own children.
- Household witchcraft will abound, relatives will not have mercy on their own family members.

- Scattered among all the nations from one end of the Earth to the other.
- No resting place for the sole of your foot.
- Anxiety of mind.
- Weariness.

- Despairing of heart.
- Dread day and night.

In the morning you will say, "If only it were evening!" and in the evening, "If only it were morning!"—because of the terror that will fill your hearts and the sights that your eyes will see.(Deut 28:67)

We all may be guilty of the above. I know of a man who begins cussing as soon as he wakes up because he is exhausted. He has sleep apnea but won't do anything about it. Personally I believe the apneic person is in captivity and may be getting choked out several times a night.

If we admit the truth, we may confess that we have wished some certain days would be over, or some weeks or months would just move along. But seriously, don't we celebrate that the year has ended every New Year's Eve. Consider if you are captive or not by your own attitude and words.

Are we being disobedient considering this verse in Matthew?

Take therefore no thought for the morrow: for the morrow shall take thought for the

things of itself. Sufficient unto the day is the
evil thereof. (Matthew 6:34)

And finally in Deuteronomy 28, Verse 68:

The Lord will send you back in ships to
Egypt on a journey I said you should never
make again. There you will offer yourselves
for sale to your enemies as male and female
slaves, but no one will buy you.

If you can't even sell yourself as a
slave, certainly you have lost all value, and
that is cursed, indeed.

Where's My Money, & *Stuff*

Not just diseases but there are other physical manifestations that can hit a person in the natural such as poverty and lack. When you are captive, you are a slave. As a slave do you get paid? Of course, not.

- Cattle and crops will be cursed. Cursed hands—nothing you try to do will work. You may come to ruin and destruction.
- Drought in the land. This was for farmers, but drought in your career is a sign of a curse. You won't enjoy the fruits of your vineyard that you planted with your own hands--, neither the fruit nor the wine of it
- Although you sow a lot of seed in the field, you won't harvest much.

- Sky becomes bronze and the earth beneath you becomes iron means prayers aren't heard, and you are not growing anything crop wise; rain of dust
- If you are being robbed, you are cursed.
- Build a house but don't get to live in it.
- Your own livestock will be killed right in front of you but you won't enjoy any of it as food.
- Strangers will eat what you work hard to produce.
- Worms will consume your plants.
- Olives will drop off your olive trees.
- Locusts will overtake your trees and crops.
- USA, stop whining. Verse 43 says that the foreigners who reside among you will rise above you higher and higher, but you will sink lower and lower. Additionally, the Curse of the Law includes a nation from far away coming in to conquer you. This is a nation whose language you don't

even understand. They will be fierce and have no mercy for the old or young. And they will consume your food and your grain. (Deuteronomy 28:49-52)

- If you are falling lower and lower, it is not the immigrant's fault—this is Biblical, it is Scriptural. America, if this is true, you are under the Curse of the Law. Repent!
- Individuals, if it looks like everybody around you is getting ahead and you're not, ask God if you are under judgment. Ask Him if you are under the Curse of the Law. Repent and come out of judgment.
- Curse of the Law: being the tail and not the head.

They will be a sign and a wonder to you and your descendants forever. Because you did not serve the Lord your God joyfully and gladly in the time of prosperity, therefore in hunger and thirst, in nakedness and dire poverty, you will serve the enemies the Lord sends against

you. He(the enemy) will put an iron yoke
on your neck until he has destroyed you.
(Deuteronomy 28:46-48)

- The cursed person will lose houses
  and lose land.

Fighting like hell all of your life to
keep a buck--, not to worship it, but just to
survive? That person is under a curse.
Devourers have been poised to take what
they get. Without Christ, there is no defense
or redemption from that curse. There is no
real help. Money is spiritual, being ripped
off is spiritual, getting delivered from being
ripped off is spiritual. Doesn't the Word say
that to spoil a house you must first bind the
strongman? That's a general rule; in order to
steal from you, you must first be bound.
Where are people bound? In captivity. In the
natural they are walking around looking like
business as usual, but in the spirit, they are
bound. It's easier for the devil to do stuff to
you if you are bound, tied up, shackle, even
padlocked.

Some may call this change in patterns
of success a downturn in business or a

reversal of fortune. Witches call it sweet pain. Some will simply *hope* for a turnaround.

This is spiritual, you had better pray. Start today. It is how you hold on to what is yours, what the Good Lord gave you. When a man does it or attempts to do it on his own this is usually when he becomes corrupt. Money is spiritual so if a person is trying to hold on to something spiritual in the flesh—there will be corruption.

If a man is trying to hold on to money, which is spiritual, by dark practices, even though that is default in the Earth, by God's standards that will lead to corruption.

A gracious woman retaineth honour: and strong men retain riches.(Proverbs 11:16)

The Lord gives us power to get wealth and power to enjoy that wealth--, that is power to keep it. All else is corruption.

That's where your money and your stuff are—in heavenly places. It would feel nice to think that God has our money and stuff for us--, and He does. But between the Third Heaven where God lives, and Earth, there is the seat of Satan in the second heaven. The second heaven is where the spiritual porch pirates live—so yes, even the stuff you don't have that is yours, actually yours—it is in heaven. It is either with God, still or it is in the other heaven, the wrong heaven if the devil has it.

Again, this is why we don't war with flesh and blood, the devil took it. He may have given it to one of his evil human agents as a reward for being evil, but it is yours. You have to take things back spiritually--, else there will be spiritual corruption. This is not how things are done. The evil human agent is already corrupt so you would have to go into the natural courts, for example to get back what belongs to you. You *may* have to go there, BUT do the spiritual work first.

Do not go to the dark kingdom to employ some evil human agent to fight the dark kingdom. Satan cannot cast out Satan. You will need to be saved, repented, and all in Christ, living upright before the Lord. then do your spiritual work.

Vengeance is the Lord's.

Don't Expect It

Flesh afflictions are seen rampantly in the Earth. This whole book was sparked by a testimony I saw online. The speaker said that the devil had most of the population on Earth under captivity. This is horrible, but it seemed horribly believable, especially as it concerns Flesh Hell. How many people are in pain, sick, languishing, dying, ill, diseased, suffering medically every day? How many ER's are there? How many pain centers are there? How many urgent care facilities are there for humans and their pets?

Beaucoup.

There are about 6,000 hospitals in the USA and they each have an emergency room. But that's not enough, is it? There are more than 10,000 free-standing urgent care centers in this country. Pets are not left out, there are more than 30,000 veterinary care centers in this country. People get sick. Am I saying that pets are captive? No, but they are sick. If you have a pet you have to know that a way to torment a person is to afflict their beloved pet. Witches do that, too.

Why are people so sick? We blame it on pollution, processed foods and Big Pharma. Sure, they may play a part in all of this but it is spiritual. Sickness, illness, and disease are all spiritual. Whether it is a fresh hell that you are experiencing or whether everyone in your family lineage suffered that same dread disease, it is spiritual. The ones that have come down your family line, if they've been in your foundation for the past three generations, they are really *in there.*

Why is it expected that old people will get sick, be sick or die sick? This is spiritual. By the time some people become elderly the flesh evidence of their captivity can be raging, while they were young, they have not even gotten a head cold. **It's spiritual.** Nothing was wrong with them all their life – so, what is this? **It's spiritual.**

I've said it before, that's not old age, that is old food--, old spiritual food, old curses, old traps and enticements that people have stepped into with no awareness that they've stepped into anything. Those are spiritual problems that they've carried all their lives that they've done nothing about either because they didn't know they had any spiritual problems or didn't know what to do about it. But now that they are old – the chicks may be coming home to roost. The time bombs may have counted all the way down, the land mines have suddenly been instructed to blow up.

When the devil doesn't let you know that he is messing with you, spiritually a person may think everything is fine. They may think everything is normal. If he just messes with you a little bit, most people chalk it up to *that's life* and live with it. It also depends on your tolerance level and expectation as to how much spiritual stuff you'll take from the devil before springing into action against him, spiritually. Messing with folks just a little bit, confuses or keeps the captive settled down so they don't think that anything is happening to them. Messing with folks makes the devil a lot of money; and it also steals God's worship when ALL of you is not serving the Lord.

How so?

You gain a few pounds, now it's time for the gym and diets and sometimes liposuction and other modalities. That costs money, and it invites more *spirits* into your life, such as *vanity*.

You get a wrinkle – do you think God made man to age and look what we call ugly when they were living to 900 years old? Beauty curses, untimely aging—now it's time for cosmetics and plastic surgery and whatever else the devil can influence a person to get. That costs money.

If the devil doesn't mark you – look at these tricks – he gets man to happily mark himself with Botox and fillers and tattoos. Once you are marked you are now a candidate or belong to the kingdom whose stuff you are using. When marked, if they— whoever stuff you are using comes for you, you can't resist. It's like being in a club in the natural and branding yourself or wearing the "team" uniform.

Blissfully doomed-, marked. The devil, who many deny that he exists, got you to do this to yourself. In a jail you are assigned a number, is it not written on the "uniform" you wear in that prison? Is this plastic surgery or a tattoo not a mark, if not *the mark of the Beast* if you are in spiritual jail and felt compelled to do it?

Now, he can leave you alone for the most part, he can toy with you a little or leave you alone completely--, if a person is already his, he can just call in the chip when he gets ready.

So a person is retired now—oh, the devil might want that person's money and retirement years so they may start getting sick. Just because you're of a certain age, don't expect it; you can live a long healthy life, until you are satisfied (Ps 91). That's not old age, that is old spiritual food, devil markers, and chips being called in. That is the culmination of all the crap the devil has done to you over the years that you ignored and did nothing about. That means you agreed with the devil.

Vanity, all is vanity says Solomon in Ecclesiastes. This may have been what he was talking about.

Too much of the world expects this and has normalized it. Surgeons make bucks off of it. Big Pharma makes *beaucoup* bucks off of it. Psychiatrists may be invoked to talk about it. It is spiritual and could have started at a person's birth. If that person is not spiritual and has not been saved all of this could have escaped him or her, as they have lived their wonderful life not knowing that they are on the way, like lambs to the slaughter. If nothing dramatic or traumatic ever happened in their life that they couldn't explain away as that's *just life,* it happened to mom or it happened to dad or grandma or grandpa this way, then most will just accept it, expect it, ignore it, live with it, die with it, or die because of it.

Without Jesus they will be shocked to their core in the end.

Soul Hell

When in Soul Hell do you dare to pray? You may not have the desire or the wherewithal to pray, but you must. The wicked jailers have authority over you in the spirit, if you are captive

Oh, you don't believe that anything spiritual is influencing you? Then when there is a move of God that comes through a man to bless a person, or a congregation, or a people or even a nation, where did that come from? I'm talking about what people call miracles and signs and wonders. It came from the spiritual realm. Hopefully it was of God, if not and you accepted a gift of any kind from the devil, you are now on the hook with the devil.

Not by power or by might, but by my Spirit says the Lord. Things start in the spirit and then they come to Earth. The dark kingdom is ever copying God so they are doing what God is doing as much as they can, even though they do counterfeit signs and wonders.

In captivity a captive is threatened with death or the death of something if they dare pray. In the natural this is the person who is afraid to pray because they think something will happen. The range can be from thinking they are so powerful and want to make sure they don't say or pray the wrong thing, to really believing that they will die if they pray.

The Lord used me to minister His Spirit to a young woman who wanted to receive the Holy Spirit, but she was scared. She really was afraid. The Lord gave me a Word of Knowledge that this woman was afraid that if she got the Holy Spirit she would die. The Lord told me to let her know that she surely would not die and had her to speak this Word:

I shall not die, but live, and declare the works of the Lord. (Psalm 118:17)

That Scripture was immediate deliverance for her. After that, she quickly received the Spirit of God, with evidence of speaking in tongues and did not die.

In Soul Hell a person is threatened in the spirit with death--, remember the person is still alive, so they may fear death. That death could be the death of the person or the death of something about that person's life. They are repressed from calling on the Name of God. Anyone who has had sleep paralysis or any kind of dream attack may have tried to call on the name of the Lord but nothing came out of their mouth. That paralysis is like a type of anesthetic that once you are "under" they can just do stuff to you. In Soul Hell there is no prayer no praise, no worship. Folks, soul hell is because of demons, devils, idols afflicting your soul, so it stands to reason that your worship would be hindered or stopped.

The captive may be isolated in the natural because if their soul is not available, if their soul is on lockdown, how will they interact with people, successfully? If you are not connected to God then there is no Fruit of the Spirit coming from you. If there is no Fruit of the Spirit, no one will really be able to stand being around you, unless they are all evil sots themselves.

Pray. You've got to pray. You've got to pray anyway – press in, even if you feel like you can't, or you shouldn't-- pray. Be sure to repent; do a prayer of repentance often, even daily. Jesus is the only way out of this imprisonment.

Prison of the souls for people who keep things in their heart and do not forgive and have bitterness (bitterness of soul), anger and other works of the flesh. You may find yourself alone in life because you are on lockdown somewhere in Soul Hell captivity. Your natural life is a manifestation of what is happening to you in the spirit. What is hidden in your heart also hides your heart from other people. When your heart is hidden, relationships cannot prosper in the natural. Unforgiveness, resentment, bitterness are evil *spirits* in the soul, blocking all your relationships, not just the one against the person you are hating on.

Soldiers who guard this jail are demons. They want you to take on their evil nature to do what they want you to do. In this level of captivity, a person will not hear the Word or repent easily. Keep trying. Keep praying.

Christians in Soul Hell have health and emotional problems because they are in league, in agreement with the devil, not Jehovah God. Soul Hell captives take it to the extreme and are even homicidal whenever they get angry.

Let all bitterness, and wrath, and anger, and clamour, and evil speaking, be put away from you, with all malice:

And be ye kind one to another, tenderhearted, forgiving one another, even as God for Christ's sake hath forgiven you. (Ephesians 4:31-32)

Call on the Name of Jesus; your life depends on it.

Spiritual Hell

Spiritual prison is also in second heaven. It is a place of the evilest retribution for serving God and warring against the dark kingdom. Warfare prayers, Fire to burn and the Blood of Jesus Christ – they hate it. And as in the natural if a policeman ever goes to jail, the inmates will despise him and attempt to attack him if they can, the jailers here hate the prayer warriors and those who genuinely serve the Lord – so be for real in your service to God and don't get captured.

Manipulations of the second heaven occurs because the *spirits* or powers of the second heaven control people on Earth who are imprisoned. Like puppets, like marionettes, when in prison, you do what the jailer says. You've heard people say you can't be in two places at once. We are learning today that you can. And, you might be amazed to find out in how many ways that can happen. You, or parts of you can be in more than two places at once.

Spiritual wickedness got a hold of a person, and they are captive in second heaven, but they are still alive here in the Earth. What is happening in the spirit in that evil kingdom then manifests in that captive person here in the natural.

People of God:

For we wrestle not against flesh and blood, but against principalities, against powers, against the rulers of the darkness of this world, against spiritual wickedness in high places. (Ephesians 6:12)

Why are you wrestling, *how* are you wrestling with those entities? It is your spirit that is *wrestling*. Wrestling implies touching – you are being **handled** when you are captured. If you don't defend yourself or attempt to get away from their holds, strongholds, chokeholds, whatever kind of holds, then you are not wrestling.

And these high places? Second heaven or other prison locations which are all hell by virtue of who the warden is and who the guards are.

These "prison guard spirits" (entities) order people to act a certain way, dress a certain way, talk a certain way and those on Earth follow what the jailer demands. What demands? Wear 8 layers of makeup. Soak in a bottle of fragrance daily. Dress like a hooker. Here's a demonic hairdo—wear that.

Saints of God, d**o not get captured.** Unrepentant sin will cause you to get captured.

Are you praying? Who is praying *for* you? Who is praying *with* you?

If you get captured, cry out for deliverance! Deliverance is the way out of captivity.

For thou wilt not leave my soul in hell; neither wilt thou suffer thine Holy One to see corruption. (Psalm 16:10, Acts 2:27)

Yes, the above verse is about Jesus, but Jesus came to show us the way. And now we know that our soul or parts of it can be in Hell then that is a very viable Word to pray for deliverance. One day I heard the quiet but audible voice of the Lord say, **"I will not leave your soul in hell."** God wasn't talking to Jesus at that time, and I wasn't eavesdropping; the Lord was talking to me.

The people in Flesh-, Soul-, or Spirit Hell are not dead; they are alive on Earth, walking out their unseen life. When the fact that they are in a living hell is not evident to them, it is **unseen**. These are the *that's life,* complacent crowd.

When there is no God in a person's life, when a person is alienated from the life of God, they don't read the Bible, they don't pray, they don't praise, or worship and they don't obey the tenets of the Gospel because they **can't**, they don't even know that what they are experiencing is not of God and they deserve better, can get better, can do better and be better. They don't know they can pray and get out of there and live an abundant life, not a bound and caged, or jailed life.

In captivity, dreams are very often wiped. The person who says, *I don't dream,* is a captive. The person who dreams but doesn't remember what they dream is a captive. The person who gets a false interpretation of their dreams is either a captive or a victim, or both and may remain captive.

You will only know what is happening to you spiritually when you are in the spirit. At night, when sleeping--, dreaming, you are in the spirit. That is your real life. That is what is really happening to you. The stuff you *will* to do in the daytime can be a whole fake life. What your spirit man is all about, what your spirit man is doing is who you really are.

Whatever demons require as they are controlling captives, that is what the prisoner must do. This is demonic possession, versus oppression. If you are captive, in jail, imprisoned, isn't the enemy in *possession* of his captive? That enemy can get you, either by influence, suggestion, their own demonic power or by force to make you do a myriad of things --, even things you don't want to do.

We have all sinned and fallen short of the glory of God. Even after salvation, we all can sin, even daily. Repent to avoid hell. Repent at all costs.

Grow in the Lord. We came into this world alone and who do you think is going with you when you go see God? You need the Word of God in you. Know the Word. *What*? You think Jesus got tested and needed the Word, but you won't, and you don't? Get real.

Minus sin, witches and satanists will leave you alone. The devil will tempt you as He did Jesus, but He won't be successful if you walk by the Spirit, live in the Word and know the Word.

Be in the right spiritual garment, be in the company of the Holy Spirit and God's ministering spirits, and the dark kingdom will leave you alone. The devil is licking his chops and counting up his victims as soon as they are captured. If you get captured, you must get out, you must break free or you will be at his mercy, and he has no mercy.

Can Your Soul Be Sold?

Can you be *nominated* for sacrifice?

Yes, evil people do it to you all the time, whether you or they realize it or not. Those who hate you are nominating you for evil. Those who are jealous of you want you to go away, sometimes permanently. Those who do not forgive you want you punished. Those who are in bitterness or resentment against you want you to suffer hurt, loss, or harmd. Those who are full on in the flesh want you dead. Whether they realize they are nominating you for sin and death or not, by their unforgiveness and having you in their head, they are wishing just that. If they are satanist they are praying that. If they are soulish, carnal, and diabolical, they are praying evil to come upon you.

Who will exact this evil?

Whether they've thought about it or not, it is the devil through one or more eil human agents. They may just think they are imagining a satisfying guilty wish against you, but really, they are invoking a demon. This could be *blind witchcraft*. It depends on who they are spiritually and how they linger on this evil *wish*. In this way they are nominating you for harm, illness, sickness, loss, or destruction.

To what degree they will continue pondering or praying this way will determine how and if this will even happen, especially if you are not prayerful. They are selling your soul or at least putting it up for sale or auction. This is all happening in the spirit, and you may not know a thing about it. This could be a relative. It could be a current friend. It could person you haven't seen in months or years, and you think that you two have gone your separate ways.

That is not always the case.

Soul tied people. Do you know people who are obsessive and just can't get over anything? We may say they are childish, no--, they are demonic. Don't cross them because that will be how they treat you as well; don't deceive yourself. This is especially dangerous and possible if the person is related to you by marriage and or is occultic. Occultic people are not amusing, they need sacrifices. Don't be their candidate.

People who are in rebellion against God are potential candidates for human sacrifice or nomination for human sacrifice.

People who are potential victims of sacrifices live in sin and are pretty much doing things that God hates, else the devil couldn't get a judgment against them and the devil couldn't receive them as a sacrifice. Yes, I'm saying that if you are walking upright before the Lord an evil human agent can't use you as sacrifice.

It is best not to hang out with known and chronic sinners, else collateral damage might be a real possibility. If a known and unrepentant sinner is your best buddy and God didn't send you to them to witness to them--, careful, if something goes down with that sinner, do you want to go down with them as collateral damage? I'm talking about more than getting caught up in a bank robbery, so the innocent driver of the car goes to jail with the actual robber. I'm talking about spiritual jail--, captivity.

This is why the Psalmist is not afraid of what man can do, those are counted as light afflictions, but if the devil has you in hell—that's when you should worry.

The Lord is on my side; I will not fear: what can man do unto me? (Psalm 118:6)

And fear not them which kill the body, but are not able to kill the soul: but rather fear him which is able to destroy both soul and body in hell. (Matthew 10:28)

What is human sacrifice? It's horrible, and it varies from being used, trafficked, enslaved, working for no wages, all the way to being made un-alive to the benefit of some other person.

Why? Why would that ever happen?

Because the demons they are serving require **blood**; the purer the blood the more they covet it. Those who are in devil contracts who are told to supply sacrifice ask for either the person that deceived person "loves" the most, or the person who loves that person the most. Depending on their demonic contract, the evil are either saving their own life by nominating another human and or they will be rewarded for doing so.

Yes, it is sick. So be careful who you love and how you think you are loving someone.

Evil human agents are the instruments on Earth that the devil uses. Satanists, magicians, witches, warlocks. Moloch rules death and murder in the Earth. It is said that the "ember" months are the rush months for blood, murder, and sacrifice. Don't be one of those; don't be a sacrifice.

- Blood of Jesus, cry for me. Anyone naming my name for sacrifice, I am not your candidate, in the Name of Jesus.
- I will live and not die, and I will declare the goodness of the Lord, in the land of the living.

If you get captured, they also capture your *stuff*. Where is your *stuff*? It is also captured. If your stuff is captured, that's a strong clue that you are as well. Answers to prayers from God must traverse the second heaven to get to us. The things and stuff that you've asked God for also must come through second heaven to get to us.

Pray your angels *through*. Be persistent in prayer so money, houses, cars and all financial things you need to function successfully in life are not porch pirated by the dark kingdom, but instead, get to you.

Prayers are also held up in the second heaven. Repent. Be fasted, pray fervently, with determination. Don't stop short or stop too soon.

Upside Down

These categories are exactly opposite or upside down in comparison to the assent into the presence of God.

A man's spirit is attacked; if he is not wise, and does not know it he won't feel it in his spirit. If he doesn't feel it soul-wise, then the results of that attack will show up in his soul. Jesus could feel spiritually; we should ascribe to that. Jesus could feel *virtue* leaving Him. It's pretty hard to feel spiritually if you are spiritually dead. Sin makes you dead, if not physically, which is what we call dead, it will make a person spiritually dead.

People moan and cry and lament and grieve all the time over their dead when they are gone physically. How many people have you heard mourn the person who is spiritually dead?

Very few, to no one.

Do we care?

Do we even know?

If a person is not aware of their spiritual death or their spiritual deadness, if they are not aware that they lost anything, that virtue was stolen from them, or that they are now different than before the attack, then the loss will remain, and the attack will continue. Not only that, sooner or later the sequela of that attack will manifest in the flesh.

We are flesh creatures, so pains and aches and issues in the flesh are what we are attuned to and spend the most time and thought, and money on.

The Devil Made Me

The devil made you do it? Yes he did. He made Eve do it, but there was still a curse for Eve. Eve got Adam to do it, and there was still a curse for Adam. And, certainly there was a curse for the Serpent.

Sadly, it is true that the devil can make you do something. When you are captive, you are like a marionette; strings are attached and you do what you are told to do, made to do. The Word says that you are bought with a price and your life is not your own when you are redeemed by Christ. The devil can entice a person to sin, but once you are in his camp, *it's on,* and not in a good way.

Of course the goal is to NEVER go there. If anyone has ever sinned with such a drive, such an urge, such a rush that they must do this thing now, or as soon as possible and with urgency? Think of rapists and murderers, who later say, *I don't know what happened.* Or, they may say, *I don't know what came over me.* They may say, *I blacked out and don't remember.* Their friends and family may say, *He would never do such a thing; he's a good person.*

Folks, that person was captive in hell and the devil decided what day, what hour, what situation he would use to detonate and make this captive do what he wanted that person to do.

Except for the prayers of the prophets, the intercessors and the saints, calling on the Lord, and the Lord's hand of protection over us all, the world would already have been lost.

That strong urge was the result of a demonic instruction and a demonic charge. If it was a sin with another person, you didn't care who the person was or what the situation was, you just felt like you **had** to do it. That shows you are (or were) in captivity and you **HAD** to do what the devil was instructing you right then. If it involved another person, that person was most likely hated by the devil, and he wanted that person attacked and or defiled. The devil used you. The devil made you. But that is not going to let you off the hook; there is much iniquity being built up against you and you will pay either now or later, or now _and_ later, unless you repent, and God completely forgives the sin, the transgression, and the iniquity.

This is why we fast. This is why we resist things. When you feel like you have to have hot wings and you get them, that is training. The devil will have you follow simple instructions first that seem as though they mean nothing. Resist the cravings and urges and serve the Lord. When you feel you must have hot wings, pray and ask the Lord, Are you instructing me to get hot wings? Do you want me to get them, even though they will raise the BP and irritate the stomach, not to mention the heat of the expulsion won't feel that great tomorrow in the toilet. Pray about it TO GOD; do not simply obey the instruction unless you know it is from God.

In that same way, when you sin, you sell your soul—to the devil and you sell it for no money and no gain. You may not even be aware that you sold it. As a puppet or a marionette, you are still not your own, you will continually be manipulated, controlled, and made to do things that you may find enjoyable at first, but eventually you will hate doing those things.

Enter the *player*. He wants to chase women, so he does. He chases so much skirt that he, in his sin, is captured, probably sooner than later. Folks, no one escapes this, no matter what they think. Then he is MADE to chase women, to sleep with them. He is made into a strange altar, he wants his narcissistic worship – from women, or whatever gender he is assigned to. He may not have an assigned gender; he may be on the *down low*. Eventually he will tire of this, he will get so tired of it, but he cannot stop. He is on assignment from hell, probably Flesh Hell. He now feels like the victim even while he is victimizing others. He is most assuredly a captive.

He will find that other parts of his life have gone lacking since the day he entered

Flesh Hell, even though he may not have known that is where he was or where he was going, or how long he would be there. All that sexual sin got him there and also kept him there. Review the curses in the life of the one who chooses sin, any and all of that could be what is happening or has happened to him. Some of it still could be in his future, if he has a living future before permanent hell.

He must repent and accept or rededicate to the Lord Jesus Christ before it is too late. He has a lot more work than that to do, getting deliverance will include breaking soul ties, breaking bondages, breaking yokes, healing his foundation, asking people for forgiveness, forgiving himself. Every time he slept with a new victim, he may have blamed the victim and so hated that person. Every time he slept with a person, he hated himself more. He has to repent of all that. But in all that hate he hasn't formed any meaningful relationships in his life. When it is all said and done, who will be with him when he needs people more than he ever has in his life?

There may be bitterness because he may not be doing well later in life, but he has no one who cares about him. That fosters more bitterness. All that hate and resentment may get him moved to Soul Hell; it depends.

Folks, this is the life of a player, we've seen it over and over for years. It is devil inspired, devil influenced, and devil directed. That man's life is stolen because of lust or his greed and desire for sexual prowess. He gained the "world" he wanted, but lost everything else including his soul. Lost souls are in Soul Hell.

Don't be that person. Even if you have made that mistake, or worse. As long as there is life, there is hope. Cry out to the Lord for deliverance.

Get Me Out of Hell

No sane person wants to miss Heaven when it is all said and done. By the same token, no sane person wants to go to hell, and especially have to spend eternity in hell. No sane person would want to spend a moment in hell, yet those who are captive are in hell—for early torment.

What?

For your consideration--, for your information and enlightenment, for your prayer life, aside from having dreams that you are actually in hell, here are some clues that you or parts of you are in hell. By hell I mean captivity, in the custody of the devil.

Whatever you sin with, the devil can very easily capture that part. It's as though you are just putting it out there like a snack.

Seriously?

- Dreams of being in captivity.
- Dreams of being in jail or in prison.

- Actually, being in jail or prison is a sign that a person started out in spiritual captivity first.
- Dreams of being in a cage or a bottle; trapped anywhere.
- Dreams of wandering and wandering, especially lost in a dark forest.
- Falling into a pit, or being in a pit.
- Dreams of trying to escape but you cannot.
- Money, financial issues.
- Health issues/hair falling out.
- One certain organ doesn't work.
- Etc.

Demonic dreams must be dealt with. If what the dream is about hasn't happened yet, then cancel the dream. If you do not cancel the dream, it says that you are in agreement with what that dream was about coming into manifestation in your life.

If your dream is notification of what you are going through in the present, then you have to pray accordingly to break that power that is controlling your life.

Jailers in the Natural

And then there are jailers in the natural, on their demonic assignment, whether they realize it or not. Mostly this book is about people who are captive and do not realize it, so they blissfully waste their life serving Satan.

I think of the person who is mean as cuss. Anybody can pick a fight, but this person is especially adept at it and fights with anyone, everyone, wherever they go. I think of the abusive spouse--, they work for Satan. The person who agrees to marry or live with this person as "significant other" will suffer their abuse and usually more and more every day. This is a tormentor and a demonic jailer in place, in person, in the physical realm to enforce the imprisonment of the person that they have "married." In interpersonal relationships, this is a *physical spirit spouse.* The person who embraces this or is willing to put up with it is spiritually imprisoned and so much so that they accept this jailer in the natural and agree to live with him (or her), feed him, sleep with him, be battered and thrown around but yet stay with him.

When one has finally had enough abuse they may run a way, or try to run away. The classic line of the *physical spirit spouse,* abuser-type man to the abused victim, who is usually a woman, is, *I will find you.* A fellow tried that with me many years ago, and now that I look back, I see he was a jailer, so was I already in captivity before I even knew it, or knew what it was? Seems I was. This guy told me that I couldn't marry anyone but him and if I tried to marry anyone else, he would come and interrupt the wedding. Folks, that was a *whole demon* talking to me and I was a 25-year-old Baptist girl then. I knew NOTHING of spiritual warfare and demons at that time.

I don't write these books for entertainment. I pray what is written in this and other books are helping people and or their children, in the Name of Jesus.

Finally, the victim is ready to get away from this "jailer", so they file civil restraining orders and or file for divorce. The problem is totally spiritual and the spiritual aspect of all of this must be dealt with FIRST.

However, if that soul is in hell, the first thing they are commanded, coerced or threatened with is praying or calling on the Name of Jesus. Usually, this most often is subconscious, unless the *physical spirit spouse* is raging, telling the person audibly not to pray, they just feel inside of them that they shouldn't pray or that prayer won't do anything, or that God doesn't care or God won't listen. None of that is true; God does care, and He hears our prayers. So, pray!

But for those who don't do the spiritual work first by praying, they may continue to seek only natural solutions to spiritual problems. You can do both, but don't neglect prayer.

This becomes clear when the divorced person meets and marries another bum just like the one they just got away from. Yes, you keep meeting the same kinds of people if you are still the same. You attract the same.

A woman married a horribly abusive man. She had several children by him. Finally, she figured out a plan and got away from him. Subsequently she met a man at work who – wow! --, had a job. As a matter of fact he had a higher position than she did. She later married that man. He is mean, foul, and abusive just like the first husband. The only difference is the second husband has a job. So the second husband is a bit more functional in his demonics. In the first marriage they fought about money a lot. This woman also worships and chases money.

Saints, this is why money is not the answer, or only money is not the answer to everything.

Okay, so in the first marriage they fought a lot, probably about everything, but mostly money. She divorces and marries a man with at least means, if not money but the torment, jailing, and even beatings continue. This woman is in captivity.

She goes to church—a good Baptist church, I'm sure where they don't do deliverance or even say the word, *deliverance*.

Anyone who takes abuse of any kind, emotional, mental, financial, physical, or sexual, on a regular basis is in captivity and their tormentor/jailer works for Satan. They are not going to just stop because you are sad, or you cry, or you are extra nice to them, or extra timid around them. They are on assignment from Satan, and they MUST torment you because they also are captive. **I bet you can see their captivity**, *but can you see your own?*

Jesus Christ is the only answer for you, them, either of you or both of you. But you cannot make that person change.

They are sent to torment you, make your life miserable. They say you can't choose family, so be sure not to choose friends unwisely. Don't marry without wise counsel. I've said it before, there are soulmates and there are roommates and there are cellmates. **But there are also jailers.**

Abusive spouses, *physical spirit spouses*, tormentors, abusive children who participate in elder abuse are tormentors and would-be jailers, if not full-blown jailers. I know of too many women especially who are afraid of their grown children.

Tormented children who torment their parents--, who started it? The devil actually, but it could be ancestral, such as ancestral drug abuse, ancestral alcoholism, money worship--, mental illness, add to that--, this is how it is in this family, they are fighting all the time. Yeah, it's *in there.*

That is not normal, it is not of God and deliverance is sorely needed.

How to Know If You Are Imprisoned

You don't have the promises of God.

You are being abused.

You are being ripped off.

You are not being emotionally supported in your life.

You may be drained in any or every way in your life.

You are in pain.

You are suffering financially or any other way.

How do you know if you are imprisoned? Sometimes and for many they don't know. Here are some clues, Do you have to fight, fight, fight for everything? You are probably in captivity. Are you rejected for no reason even when you meet brand new people? Are you hated, stared at, treated poorly even though you are being as respectful, kind, and nice as you can be?

You are most likely marked with a mark because you are in captivity. Mankind is not designed to live this life in captivity--, that's not really living.

Are you living an abundant life? The life Jesus said we should have? Are you redeemed from death? From sickness? (God said He'd put none of the diseases on you that He put on the Egyptians.) If you are even worried about any of these things, it means that you are not living the *abundant life.*

Have you **chosen** life? Or have you chosen death?

The goal of many jailers is to not let you know that you are captive, you're so much easier to manage that way. Some of this is answered in my book, **Has My Soul Been Sold**? A sold soul, if it is still alive, is captive. The devil is either ready to sell it again, keep it captive, or kill it. Steal, kill, destroy, that's all the devil is about.

REPENT. Daily.

The devil can sell a soul and still own it – because what you will be doing as a sold soul is devil work. It will still be evil, and he will still be deriving benefit from you. Plus, the person buying it will never pay the devil back. It is idiotic to think that the devil is a good person to go into business with. So, in the natural there are people who act just like the devil – they are jailers. Many entice you to sin so they can capture you or they've been both instructed and empowered to do so... a sold soul is one that can also be a jailer. He or she thinks they are being promoted—is a promotion into more evil really a promotion? Ultimately that is a demotion because the judgement will be so harsh, so much harsher.

Your dream life is your spirit life and it is your real life. I say that because you may be in flesh for 100 years or so, while you've been a spirit from the beginning and will remain a spirit throughout eternity and to infinity. Your dream state is very important so pay close attention to what happens in that world.

How Did I Get Here?

How does one get into captivity?

- Ancestors.
- Parents.
- Sin.

Sin includes love of the world. The devil took Jesus upon a high place and showed Him the world and said that he'd give that all to Jesus if Jesus would fall down and worship him. Jesus refused the world, so should we.

Secular music makes us sing and tap our toes where we agree with unscriptural, unbiblical and ungodly lyrics--, most often, unaware that we are doing it. **STOP IT!** Oh you just want to fit in? Why? We are to be in the world and not *of* it; instead, just passing through. Why is it so important for the world to like you or accept you? It's the world, for crying out loud. If God sent you into it, go there and witness and win souls, else, there is nothing there for you.

Jesus said, **Marvel not that they hate you; they hated Me first.**

Other ways people become captive:

- Generational curses.
- Familial curses.
- Witchcraft.
- Occultic nomination.
- Entrapment.
- Enticement.
- Ignorance.
- Initiation
- Indoctrination
- False teachers
- False prophets
- False pastors – can you imagine the folks who have followed fake pastors into hell? Permanently?
- Collective captivity
- Collateral captivity – in the wrong place, with the wrong people at the most inopportune time.

There are so many ways; broad is the way to hell, even the hells for the living.

How to Get Out

Oh that men would praise the Lord for his
goodness, and for his wonderful works to
the children of men!

For he hath broken the gates of brass, and
cut the bars of iron in sunder. (Psalm
107:15-16)

Praise is a way to get out of captivity;
it worked for Paul and Silas who were
praising God at midnight when the prison
doors opened. Praise is of course a result of
being broken out of jail, but intense, focused
praise and worship can break the bars of iron,
even it they are spiritual bars. This will break
you out of strongholds.

Fools because of their transgression, and
because of their iniquities, are afflicted.

Their soul abhorreth all manner of meat;
and they draw near unto the gates of death.
(Psalm 107:17-18)

Fools despise instruction and will go along in life the way they want to instead of the way God says. Those are the ones who get captured. I may not be talking about any contemporary person, but perhaps an ancestor is the reason you may be in captivity. You may be innocent of any transgression but instead you may be paying the price imposed by the devil for the ancestor who made a devil deal and lived their own life very large while the generations pay his or her spiritual debt.

Repent for that person. Getting angry with them now won't help, it will actually make matters even worse. Anger, especially constant or chronic anger lands a person in Soul Hell. As well long-standing anger leads to bitterness – more Soul Hell.

But when we finally realize that we are in hell, we may and should cry out to the Lord for deliverance.

Then they cry unto the Lord in their
trouble, and he saveth them out of their
distresses.
He sent his word, and healed them, and
delivered them from their destructions.
Oh that men would praise the Lord for his
goodness, and for his wonderful works to
the children of men! (Psalm 107: 19-21,
emphasis, mine)

Cry out to the Lord for deliverance. If
you don't know what to say or what to pray,
you can find deliverance Scriptures in the
Bible; many are in the Psalms.

But do thou for me, O God the Lord, for thy
name's sake: because thy mercy is good,
deliver thou me.
For I am poor and needy, and my heart is
wounded within me.
I am gone like the shadow when it
declineth: I am tossed up and down as the
locust.
My knees are weak through fasting; and my
flesh faileth of fatness.
I became also a reproach unto them: when
they looked upon me they shaked their
heads.
Help me, O Lord my God: O save me
according to thy mercy:

That they may know that this is thy hand;
that thou, Lord, hast done it.
Let them curse, but bless thou: when they
arise, let them be ashamed; but let thy
servant rejoice. (Psalm 109:21-29)

People of God, get out of captivity as soon as you become aware of it, else your entire life could be wasted and stolen from you. All that time you thought you were your own man, doing your own thing, the captain of your own ship, only to find out you didn't even have a ship is quite devastating. It is all vanity. We do not want our life to boil down to *all is vanity, meaning all is useless and worthless.*

Furthermore, you need to deal with spiritual matters while you are young. Learn all you can, do all you can and do all you should because when you get old, if you were not spiritual, do you think your kids will be? And what will they know? Will they know what you are talking about if you tell them spiritual things that are happening to you that you don't even know how to describe? Who in your household will know how to pray for you or with you?

Maybe no one, they may just say, grandma or grandpa is talking crazy again, while you need to get out of whatever living hell you may be in as you finally become aware of it.

Look at all you would have lost in life, time, family, finances – and there at the end, will you have any good legacy, any good thing, any good inheritance to leave to your children or your *children's* children? None, if it all has been stolen from you while you were in the world, blissfully in captivity and like a slave working for the devil.

Get out of captivity and hell now,. Today. At least start working on it today by calling on the Name of the Lord and becoming sincere and diligent in prayer and the disciplines of the Faith. Don't gauge if your life is going correctly by what the Jones' are doing or what they have; they are the world. What does God say you should be, be doing, and have?

Early I will destroy all the wicked of the land, That I may cut off all the evildoers from the city of the Lord. (Psalm 101:8)

How to Know That You are Out

Call on the Lord; He will deliver. He is the only one who can get you out of the hell of captivity. No matter where you're captive, no matter when you got there. As long as you are still alive in the natural, you can be redeemed from hell. But you must pray. You must be serious. You must really want out. You must serve the Lord, and be *all in*.

When good things finally start happening on a regular basis in your life then you will know that you are living the abundant life.

When all these blessings and curses I have set before you come on you and you take them to heart wherever the Lord your God disperses you among the nations, and when you and your children return to the Lord your God and obey him with all your heart and with all your soul according to everything I command you today,

then the Lord your God will restore your fortunes and have compassion on you and gather you again from all the **nations** where he scattered you. (Deuteronomy 1:1-3, *emphasis, mine*)

So, if you've been restored to your former glory, or something better, then you know that you are out of captivity. There are conditions to getting out of captivity and staying out of captivity. That should be easy to understand because they are the same conditions required to not get captured in the first place. Obey the Lord God and His commandments with all your heart and with all your soul.

As you see in the next verse, even if you have been banished to a most distant land under the heavens, God will gather you back again.

You may not have been fully aware that you went on a journey or even a far journey, but I find this wording very interesting, *"to a most distant land under the heavens."* I believe the writer is speaking of regions in second heaven, where the seat of Satan is. He is writing about regions in spiritual places, *regions of captivity.* Recall, captivity can be in parts and imprisonment could be in a prison for the flesh, a prison for the soul, or a prison of the spirit.

Even if you have been banished to the most distant land under the heavens, from there the Lord your God will gather you and bring you back. (Deuteronomy 1:4)

The Lord will bring you back out of captivity and change your heart to a heart that will obey Him. He will renew your spirit, creating a right spirit in you. The Lord will also make you prosperous, or prosperous again (v.9) so that everything you set your hands to, will be a success (v. 9)

When your life starts going right, shall you not know it? When good things start happening in your life again and on a steady and regular basis you will know that your captivity is over. Just reverse all the curses from Deuteronomy and compare with the blessings to see if you are receiving from the Lord. If you are then you are in right alignment with God. If you are, then you are definitely out of prison, out of captivity.

People of God, you will just feel better, if I can say that. The oppressive, heavy feelings will be gone. You may feel lighter, happier. Glad to wake up in the morning instead of spitting nails as soon as you open your eyes. You will feel like you are actually living and not just existing or trudging through life.

Instead of the thorn shall come up the fir tree, and instead of the brier shall come up the myrtle tree: and it shall be to the LORD for a name, for an everlasting sign that shall not be cut off. (Isaiah 55:13)

Prevention

Don't sin. Sin not. Repent often and quickly. Repent of the sins of your parents and ancestors, at least 10 generations back. I personally go all the way back to Adam and Eve.

Worldliness won't keep you out of captivity; it is what will get you in. Being a carnal Christian or a Christian in name only, a CINO, won't prevent your being captured. The devil is not only looking for people to capture, but he is also sending enticements, entrapments, even placing snacks in his traps to capture folks.

The same stuff that will get you out, will keep you out. So, if you were ever captured and got out, remember what and *Who* brought you out and keep worshipping with all your might, with all your heart and soul.

You might complain that Job did all he could, and he was still tormented and attacked. True, but Job didn't have the Holy Spirit or the Better Covenant, or the Blood of Jesus. Old Testament salvation was by works, not by Grace through Faith.

We have so many more advantages spiritually speaking. Did Job have a written Bible? Did Job have the Bible in so many translations? Did Job have a Strong's Concordance and all the other study tools that we have?

Did Job have the modern conveniences that we enjoy that save us time? You know, that time that we should be using to read and study the Word of God. And that time that we could be using in prayer and warfare? Had Jesus died for Job? In the scheme of spiritual things, He had because the Lamb was slain before the foundation of the world, but did Job know that?

No, Job didn't even know who his opponent was. He thought that God was doing all this stuff to him. We know who our enemy is; shall we war? Shall we fight? Or shall we remain captive and just party like the world, like lambs going to slaughter with no clue of what is happening to them? Shall we not contest the doom that the enemy has planned for us? Yes, we will fight. We must contest this captivity.

We know that we have an enemy and we know who he is, therefore, let us stand and stand, therefore. Let us believe the Word of God because it is true. Let us go past that "tree" that we are not supposed to eat of. But if we happen to stop by that tree, let us not look on that fruit. If we look on that fruit, let us not touch it. If we touch it, let us not take it. If we take it, let us not taste it. If we taste it--, Lord, let us spit it out of our mouth immediately, and repent.

- Lord, help us; help us all. Please, in the Name of Jesus.

I wrote the above just that way to make us aware that there are many steps to sin and many opportunities to shun it or resist it, or flee from it. But sin is done by invitation, which you may know I call *sinvitation*, and sin is accomplished with a demonic charge and demonic escort. So by the time you are in the process of sinning you feel compelled to do this thing that you are doing. It's as though you feel you have to do it. That is captivity. I have felt that feeling before and I am not proud to say that I have sinned and fallen short of the glory of God--, and more than once. Lord, please forgive; thank God for repentance and being redeemed back into right relationship with the Lord God.

Urges to sin, lusting to sin--, these are all programmed evils in those who are captive. They are captive, they must sin. Sadly, sin is what got them where they are.

Our only hope is Jesus Christ.

AMEN.

Dear Reader:

Captivity is hell. Even though captivity is spiritual, it is literally hell. Parts of you could be imprisoned, spirit, soul, or body. Don't accept any bondage or spiritual imprisonment. Mostly because you belong to God and should not be in a satanic lock up of any kind, but also because your natural life will be disastrous if your spiritual life is on lockdown.

Thank you for acquiring and reading this book. I pray it has been a blessing to you and will change how you see and do things, spiritually, for the better.

In the Name of Jesus,

AMEN.

Dr. Marlene Miles

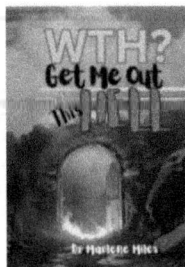

Mentioned and related titles:

Spirit of Death & the Grave, Pass Over Me and My House https://a.co/d/7ZSH406

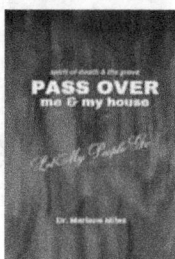

Caged Life: Get out Alive https://a.co/d/hOO8WDE

Players Gonna Play https://a.co/d/bOc3Jig

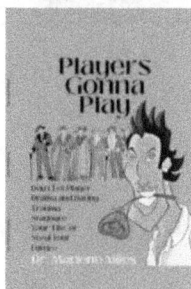

Has My Soul Been Sold? https://a.co/d/6CyxDno

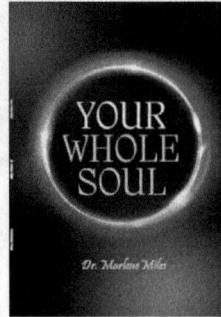

Your Whole Soul https://a.co/d/gLRMlmr

The Unseen Life https://a.co/d/21FqCos

Other books by this author

Do Not Swear by the Moon

Don't Refuse Me, Lord (4 book series)

https://a.co/d/idP34LG

Dream Defilement

The Emptiers: *Thieves of Darkness, 1*
https://a.co/d/5I4n5mc

Evil Touch

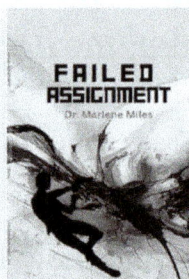

Failed Assignment

Fantasy Spirit Spouse
https://a.co/d/hW7oYbX

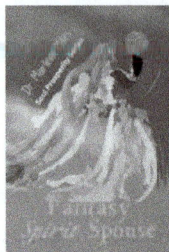

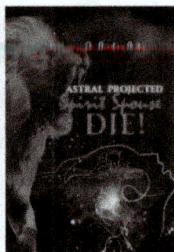

FAT Demons (The): *Breaking Demonic Curses*

The Fold (5-book series)

- The Fold (Book 1)
- Name Your Seed (Book 2)
- The Poor Attitudes of Money (3)
- Do Not Orphan Your Seed (4)
- For the Sake of the Gospel (5)
- My Sowing Journal

Gang Ups: Touch Not God's Anointed

got HEALING? Verses for Life

got LOVE? Verses for Life

got HOPE? Verses for Life

got money? https://a.co/d/g2av41N

Has My Soul Been Sold?

How to Dental Assist

How to Dental Assist2: Be Productive, Not Wasteful

I Take It Back

Legacy

Let Me Have A Dollar's Worth
https://a.co/d/h8F8XgE

Level the Playing Field

Living for the NOW of God

Lose My Location
https://a.co/d/crD6mV9

Man Safari, *The*

Marriage Ed. Rules of Engagement & Marriage

Made Perfect in Love

Money Hunters: Beware of Those

Money on the Altar https://a.co/d/4EqJ2Nr

Mulberry Tree https://a.co/d/9nR9rRb

Motherboard (The) - *Soul Prosperity Series*

Name Your Seed

Occupy: *Until I Return*

Plantation Souls

Players Gonna Play

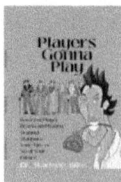

Power Money: Nine Times the Tithe

https://a.co/d/gRt41gy

The Power of Wealth *(forthcoming)*

Powers Above

The Robe, Part 1, The Lessons of Joseph

The Robe, Part II, The Lessons of Joseph

Seasons of Grief

Seasons of Waiting

Seasons of War

Second Marriage, Third--, *Any Marriage*

https://a.co/d/6m6GN4N

Sift You Like Wheat

Six Men Short: What Has Happened to all the Men?

Soul Prosperity soul prosperity series 3

https://a.co/d/5p8YvCN

Souls Captivity soul prosperity series 2

The Spirit of Poverty

StarStruck

SUNBLOCK

The Swallowers: *Thieves of Darkness*, 3

Take It Back

This Is NOT That: How to Keep Demons from Coming at You

Time Is of the Essence

Too Many Wives: *Why You Have Lady Problems*

Tormenting Spirits
https://a.co/d/dAogEJf

Toxic Souls

Triangular Power *(series)*

- Powers Above
- SUNBLOCK
- Do Not Swear by the Moon
- STARSTRUCK

Uncontested Doom

Unguarded Hours, *The*

Unseen Life, *The* (forthcoming)

Upgrade: How to Get Out of Survival Mode

- Toxic Souls (Book 2 of series)
- Legacy (Book 3 of series)

The Wasters: *Thieves of Darkness,* Bk 2

https://a.co/d/bUvI9Jo

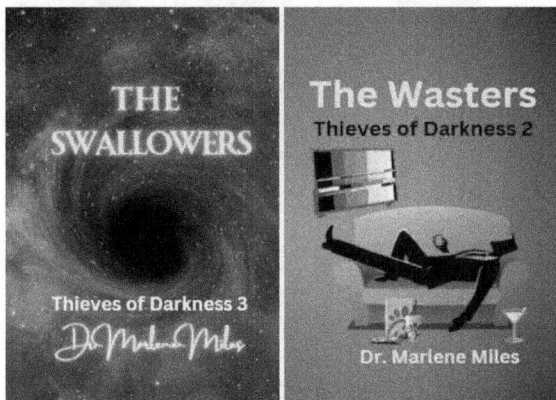

What Have You to Declare? What Do You Have With You from Where You've Been?

When I Was A Child, *I Prayed As a Child*

When the Devourer is Rebuked

https://a.co/d/1HVv8oq

The Wilderness Romance *(series)* This series is about conducting a Godly relationship and marriage with someone who is a Wilderness person. It is about how to recognize it and navigate through it. These books are about how not to get caught up in such.

- *The Social Wilderness*
- *The Sexual Wilderness*

- *The Spiritual Wilderness*

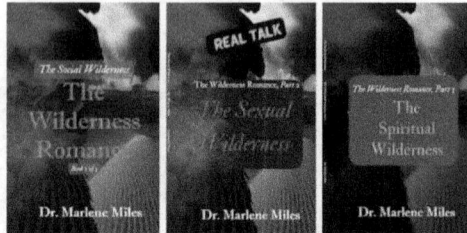

WTF? Get Me Out of This HELL

Other Series

The Fold (a series on Godly finances)
https://a.co/d/4hz3unj

Soul Prosperity Series https://a.co/d/bz2M42q

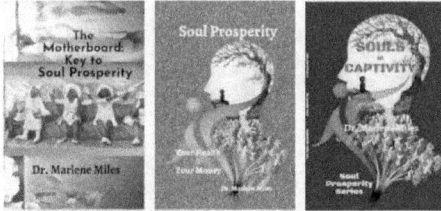

Spirit Spouse books https://a.co/d/9VehDSo

https://a.co/d/97sKOwm

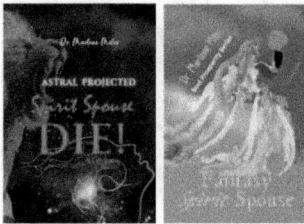

Thieves of Darkness series

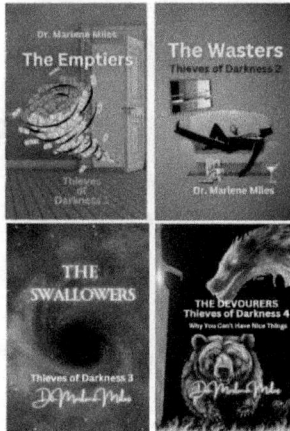

Triangular Powers https://a.co/d/aUCjAWC

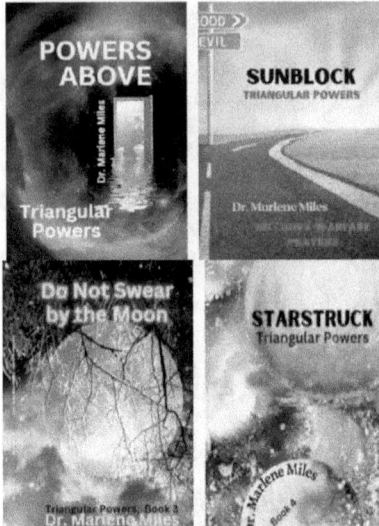

Upgrade (series) *How to Get Out of Survival Mode*
https://a.co/d/aTERhX0

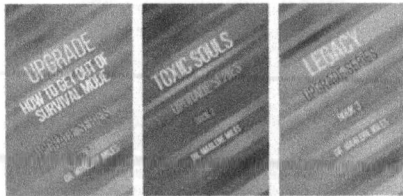